Texas Joins the United States

P.O. Box 196 • Hockessin, Delaware 19707

Titles in the Series

Texas Joins
the United States

Russell Roberts

Printing   1   2   3   4   5   6   7   8   9

Library of Congress Cataloging-in-Publication Data
Roberts, Russell, 1953–
    Texas joins the United States / by Russell Roberts.
        p. cm.—(Building America)
    Includes bibliographical references and index.
    Audience: Grades 7-8.
    ISBN 978-1-58415-550-8 (library bound)
    1. Texas—History—Revolution, 1835–1836—Juvenile literature. 2. Texas—History—Republic, 1836–1846—Juv-enile literature. 3. Texas—History—1846–1950—Juvenile literature. I. Title.
F390.R63 2008
976.4'03—dc22

                                                                        2007023490

ABOUT THE AUTHOR: Russell Roberts has written and published nearly 40 books for adults and children on a variety of subjects, including baseball, memory power, business, New Jersey history, and travel. He has written numerous books for Mitchell Lane Publishers, including *Nathaniel Hawthorne, Thomas Jefferson, Holidays and Celebrations in Colonial America, Daniel Boone,* and *The Lost Continent of Atlantis.* He lives in Bordentown, New Jersey, with his family and a fat, fuzzy, and crafty calico cat named Rusti.

PHOTO CREDITS: Cover, pp. 1, 3—North Wind Picture Archives; p. 6—Texas State Library and Archives Commission; p. 12—David A. Hayes; p. 14—Jonathan Scott; p. 17— Dr. Antonio Rafael de la Cova; p. 20—Library of Congress; p. 38—University of Texas; p. 22— J. Williams; p. 27—Texas State Library and Archives Commission; p. 28—State Preservation Board; pp. 30, 32—Barbara Marvis; p. 36—Concord Coach

PUBLISHER'S NOTE: This story is based on the author's extensive research, which he believes to be accurate. Documentation of such research is contained on page 46.
    The internet sites referenced herein were active as of the publication date. Due to the fleeting nature of some web sites, we cannot guarantee they will all be active when you are reading this book.

Contents

*For Your Information

At the Battle of San Jacinto, Texas won its independence from Mexico. The battle lasted less than thirty minutes.

Chapter

The Battle of San Jacinto

It was 4:30 in the afternoon on April 21, 1836. The 1,250 Mexican troops under Mexico's dictatorial president, General Antonio López de Santa Anna, were relaxing on marshy ground adjacent to the San Jacinto River in southeast Texas. Santa Anna had decided that since the ragtag Texas army had not attacked earlier, they were not likely to do so at all that day. He was resting in his tent. Some reinforcement troops were resting too—lying down, sleeping, sitting on the ground, or eating. Many of the Mexican troops were taking a siesta—their traditional afternoon nap. The entire army had recently marched many miles from Mexico, fought and won a bloody battle at the Alamo in the Texas city of San Antonio de Béxar, and then marched across most of Texas in pursuit of the rebel government and its disorganized army. There was a fight coming with the Texian army, and they wanted to be strong. Santa Anna was confident that it just wouldn't be today.

Meanwhile, the knee-high grass rustled and swayed on a flat plain facing the Mexican camp, as hundreds of Texian soldiers hurried silently forward toward the Mexican army.

Santa Anna had already decided that the Texas army, numbering about 800 men under the command of Sam Houston, posed little threat to him. Indeed, the Texians had been steadily retreating east across Texas in the face of the superior Mexican forces. It would later be called the Runaway Scrape, this racing retreat across the heartland of Texas by the tiny Texian army and hundreds of other people who abandoned their homes in the face of the approaching Mexicans. Santa Anna had already massacred the defenders of the Alamo, while another Mexican army had executed in cold blood hundreds of Texian soldiers at the town of Goliad, and no one wanted to wait around and find out what the Mexicans would do next.

"People and things were all mixed, and in confusion," said a slave on the run. "The children were crying, the women praying and the men cursing. I tell you it was a serious time."[1]

Seeing the frightened Texians and their army scramble helter-skelter to get out of his way, Santa Anna felt he had little to fear from these scared rebels. They had started this fight, battling Mexican authority and declaring independence for the Mexican territory of Texas, and he was determined to finish it.

The Texas powder keg, which had been threatening to ignite for several years, had exploded at the end of 1835. The Texians had won a few battles against Mexican forces, and had thought independence was practically assured—but that was before Santa Anna had arrived from Mexico City with his veteran troops. In mid-February he had crossed into Texas with his army, determined to put down the rebellion quickly. After destroying the Alamo garrison, he had marched across Texas in pursuit of the rebel government, which hopped from town to town like a frightened frog to escape him. With the rest of Texas tripping all over itself to get out of his way, Santa Anna felt that he was on the verge of a decisive victory.

Santa Anna was confident after the Alamo, so he had divided his army of several thousand into three groups. Some went south toward Goliad, others north. He went with the center group, chasing both the rebel government and Houston's army across Texas. Santa Anna believed he had little to fear from Houston, who some speculated was heading all the way east, out of Texas and into Louisiana in the United States, where he hoped to pick up more volunteer soldiers and return to Texas to continue the fight.

On April 15, Santa Anna had burned the home of Texas's government, a tiny settlement near San Jacinto called Harrisburg, which the rebel government had abandoned only a day before. On April 20, he had burned the most recent seat of Texas's insurgent government, a tiny town called New Washington. In fact, his advance troops had missed capturing fleeing members of the government by just minutes. The Texians were indeed on the run.

Santa Anna had nothing but contempt for the Texas forces. His troops were trained and disciplined—battle-hardened soldiers. The Texians were, as one member of their army described them, " . . . all unwashed, unshaven for months, their long hair, beard and mustaches, ragged and matted, their clothes in tatters, and plastered with mud."[2] An unruly and barely disciplined mob; Santa Anna was confident that he would have little trouble with them. He knew the Texian army was in front of him, and he had spent the night of the 20th and morning of the 21st supervising the building of barricades. But when the Texas army seemed in no mood to fight that day, Santa Anna let his guard down, and the entire Mexican camp did the same.

So, in the late afternoon of April 21, the Napoleon of the West—as Santa Anna liked to think of himself—relaxed along with his troops. According to local legend, Santa Anna shared his tent that afternoon with Emily West, a free black woman. That is why, the legend says, he was so unprepared for what was about to happen.

At 4:30 P.M., the calm in the Mexican camp was shattered by several bursts of grapeshot from the Texians' cannon. The onrushing Texas army stopped about forty yards from the Mexicans and delivered their first and only concentrated volley of gunfire into the bewildered camp. Then, with Texas Secretary of War Thomas Rusk shouting, "If we stop, we are cut to pieces! Don't stop—go ahead—give them Hell!"[3] 800 furious Texians swarmed into the Mexican camp like a deadly whirlwind. They shouted: "Remember the Alamo, [and] Goliad"[4] as they tore into the Mexicans with knives, clubs, hatchets, and pistols.

9

It was a slaughter—hundreds of individual fights instead of a regular battle between armies. Against the white-hot fury of the Texians, experts in hand-to-hand combat, the superior discipline of the Mexican army counted for nothing. The Texians wanted vengeance, and they got it. They shot, clubbed, and stabbed the frightened Mexicans to death as they desperately tried to surrender.

"The most awful slaughter I ever saw was when the Texans pursued the retreating Mexicans, killing on all sides, even the wounded,"[5] said a Texian soldier who participated in the fight.

Within eighteen minutes the battle was over. Six hundred and fifty Mexicans had been killed, and another seven hundred or so had been taken prisoner. Nine Texians were killed.

Santa Anna, who had rushed from his tent and run about the camp wringing his hands at the first sounds of battle, escaped from the camp on horseback. However, he was captured the next day by a Texas patrol. Wearing old clothes he had stolen from a cabin, his identity was unknown to the Texas patrol until he was brought back to camp. There, Mexican soldiers began calling his name, and the Texians realized that they had captured the Napoleon of the West.

Santa Anna was taken to General Sam Houston, who was lying under an oak tree because of a wound to his ankle. "Tell General Houston that I am tired of blood and war, and have seen enough of this country to know that the two people can not live under the same laws," he said. "And I am willing to treat with him as to the boundaries of the two countries."[6]

This was an incredible statement, considering that just a few days before, Santa Anna had been determined to wipe out the Texas rebellion. Houston, knowing that Santa Anna was worth more alive than dead, ignored the obvious falsehood and began negotiations with the defeated ruler. These soon resulted in the much-cherished goal of Texas independence.

The Texians had won their independence. But in the afterglow of victory, the question quickly became: What now?

Santa Anna

Antonio López de Santa Anna

He could have been one of the greatest leaders in Mexican history, but in the end, his own blind ambition and vanity caused him to become just another failed dictator.

Antonio López de Santa Anna Pérez de Lebrón was born to a middle-class family on February 21, 1794, in Jalapa, Veracruz. In 1810, he was appointed a cadet in an infantry regiment, thus beginning his long military career.

Early on Santa Anna was loyal to Spain, which controlled Mexico. Then in 1821, showing a tendency that he would exhibit all his life, Santa Anna abruptly switched sides and began fighting with the Mexican insurgent leader, Agustín de Iturbide. When Iturbide won and later became emperor, he rewarded Santa Anna with a promotion to general. Yet just two years later, Santa Anna was part of a group that overthrew Iturbide and established a Mexican republic.

In 1829, Santa Anna's popularity soared when he defeated a Spanish invasion force that was trying to recapture Mexico. In 1833, he was elected president of Mexico. He gradually consolidated his power and became a dictator.

Santa Anna will forever be remembered in American history for his role at the Alamo. However, his defeat at the Battle of San Jacinto on April 21, 1836, gained Texas its independence.

Back home in Mexico, Santa Anna played a game of musical chairs with the Mexican presidency. Kicked out after his defeat at San Jacinto, he redeemed himself during a subsequent military campaign against the French, and by 1841 was president again. Four years later he was overthrown, only to be recalled for service against the invading Americans during the Mexican War. With the army behind him, he declared himself president once again. After losing to the Americans, he fled to Jamaica in 1847.

In 1853, Santa Anna returned to Mexico and once more became dictator. By 1855, he had again worn out his welcome, and was overthrown for the final time. While living in exile in New York City, he imported the first shipments of chicle to America. Chicle became the foundation of the chewing gum industry.

Santa Anna died on June 21, 1876, in Mexico City.

FYI For Your Information

Aaron Burr was a soldier, lawyer, United States Senator, and vice president of the United States. He became infamous when he mortally wounded Alexander Hamilton in a duel. In 1805, Burr and James Wilkinson conspired to establish an empire in Louisiana and Texas. Wilkinson revealed the plot to President Thomas Jefferson, and Burr was tried for treason. He was acquitted.

Chapter

Men Without A Country

Philip Nolan could be considered the patron saint of all those who came to Texas in the first two decades of the 1800s. Nolan was a real man whose life was greatly fictionalized in the famous novel *The Man Without a Country*. Born in Ireland in 1771, Nolan represented General James Wilkinson's business interests in New Orleans in the late 1780s. There he first learned of opportunities in the land just beyond the western border of Louisiana—a land of vast, wide-open spaces, untamed and wild, with just a few towns, where a person could go for hours or even days without seeing another living soul. It was a place called Texas, a Spanish possession, and Nolan was one of the first to hear its siren song of unlimited land, freedom from authority, and opportunity.

Nolan took several trips into Texas, gathering wild mustangs and other goods. Unfortunately for him, he also aroused the suspicions of Spanish authorities, who were always on the alert for individuals taking advantage of Texas's vastness. Maybe Nolan was just a trader . . . or maybe he had dreams of empire. Whatever it was, on March 21, 1801, Nolan was killed in a battle with Spanish soldiers.

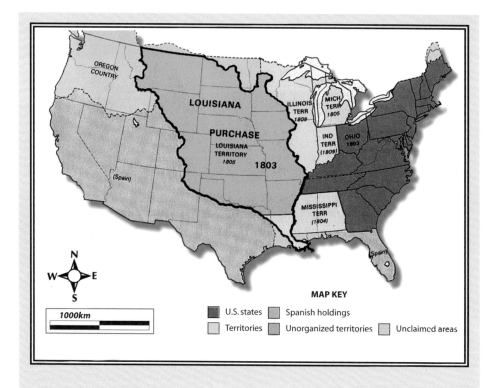

The United States in 1810. Almost all of Texas was initially under Spanish control. Mexico took over when it won its independence from Spain in 1812.

Nolan's unfortunate end did nothing to discourage others from looking at Texas and seeing their own glory reflected in it. This became especially true after 1803, when the Louisiana Purchase put United States soil right alongside Texas. Suddenly, the expansionist-minded Americans, who had already pushed westward into Illinois, Ohio, and Michigan, were on the doorstep of Texas.

Spain had watched with alarm as the spirit of revolution and freedom that America had let loose with its victory over England in the War for Independence had swept over Europe. France's monarchy had already fallen victim to a revolution. Now these same democracy-loving Americans were poised to bring their ideas of representative government into sparsely settled Texas, where only an estimated 3,500 people lived.

In 1806, Aaron Burr, a former vice president of the United States, headed an expedition that was supposedly going to carve an empire out of parts of the yet-unformed states of Louisiana and Texas.[1] It failed, but it heralded what was to come.

After that, Texas constantly seemed to be on the minds of men who dreamed of power and glory. Augustus W. Magee, José Bernardo Maximiliano Gutiérrez de Lara, Warren D. C. Hall, Henry Perry, Jean Robert Marie Humbert, John Robinson, Louis Michel Aury, Dr. James Long . . . all these at one time or another in the first two decades of the 1800s planned ambitious military invasions of Texas. They all had the ultimate goal of wresting Texas from Spain's grip and setting themselves up as ruler of a new empire. All came to grief, their hopes dying bitter deaths because of failed planning, disruption by Spanish forces, their own inflated sense of self-worth, and general ineptitude.

Besides dreams of empire, the other reason men were attracted to Texas was simply the land. It was almost mind-boggling in size— approximately 265,000 square miles. Although parts were rocky, dry and wind-swept, the lands of eastern Texas near the Gulf of Mexico were so rich and fertile that giant canebrakes would grow from nothing to twenty-five feet high every year, then collapse from the sheer monstrous size, only to do it again the next year.

In 1819, Spain had reason to hope that perhaps American adventures in Texas were over. In that year, the Adams-Onís Treaty surrendered any U.S. claims to Texas in return for Florida—itself a big piece of real estate. But Spain's hopes of relief were quickly dashed by the outcry over the treaty in America. Sure, people said, Florida was nice, but we want Texas, too. So Spain waited and held its breath.

A hostile takeover of Texas was the last thing the destitute Moses Austin desired in 1820. He had in mind a different type of invasion—one that swapped fighting for friendship and traded arms for allegiance.

Austin was one of the many men who looked at Texas and saw opportunity. However, unlike those before him, Moses did not want to

15

ride into Texas at the head of an army of conquerors. Instead, his idea was to gain power in Texas by bringing in families loyal to Spain to colonize the region. This would remove one of the major incentives to future revolutionaries—Texas's vast openness, which just begged someone to come along and try to establish their own empire in it. In return for being welcomed with open arms by Spanish authorities, Austin imagined that he would become the leader of the colony.

As Austin thought, Spanish authorities embraced his plan. "Raise your spirits. Times are changing. A new chance presents itself,"[2] he wrote hopefully to his son Stephen. But before Moses could take advantage of this new opportunity, he died on June 10, 1821.

It fell to Stephen, a failed mine-owner and merchant, to pick up the Texas torch that his father had dropped. In July 1821, he placed an advertisement for 300 families to get the ball rolling, and then splashed over the Sabine River (the border between Louisiana and Texas) and headed to the little town of San Antonio de Béxar, the Texas capital.

When he arrived, on August 12, he was greeted with the stunning news that Mexico had won its independence from Spain. That could have ended the whole arrangement right there, but fortunately the new Mexican authorities honored Austin's existing agreement. In return for a generous land grant—over 1,000 acres in many cases—a family had to observe the Catholic religion, swear allegiance to Mexico, and be honest and hardworking farmers. In other words, they could be power-hungry zealots determined to start a new empire.

Initially, Austin had reluctantly taken over his father's scheme. But as he rode over the boundless Texas countryside, trying to decide where to place his settlers, he found himself falling under the spell of Texas that had bewitched so many before him. "[T]he idea of contributing to fill it [Texas] with a civilized and industrious population filled my soul with enthusiasm,"[3] he said.

He also enthusiastically noted the richness of the land: "This land is very productive and is covered with the most luxuriant growth of grass I ever beheld in any country."[4]

Stephen Austin was the father of Texas. Although this pose shows him grabbing a rifle, he was a diplomat, not a soldier.

Austin was the first Texas *empresario*—someone who signed a contract with the Mexican government to bring settlers into Texas. Upon his return to Louisiana, Austin found that his advertisement had generated almost 100 replies from people eager to relocate to Texas. Soon a steady stream of wagons was moving through Natchitoches, a town in Louisiana close to the Texas border, all filled with families eager for a fresh start in life. The attraction was land—plenty of it, and cheap. For the same amount that it would cost a person to buy 80 acres of fertile plantation ground in the southern United States, a Texas settler could acquire 4,428 acres.

The exodus to Texas had begun.

Austin's idea had been sound, and thanks to his rigorous screening process, most of his initial 300 families (known as the Old Three Hundred in Texas history, although the actual number was 297) were exactly the type of loyal, hardworking people that the Mexican government desired. Austin and his families settled in an area of approximately 15,000 square miles—an enormous space, but one that barely made a dent in the great emptiness of Texas. With just two towns—San

Antonio de Béxar and Goliad, and one other nearly abandoned community, Nacogdoches—Texas was a waiting vessel ready to be filled.

Drought, a bad harvest, Indian troubles, and a long period spent by Austin in far-off Mexico City almost destroyed the colony in its first year. Some gave up and returned to the United States. But Austin's return stabilized the colony, and gave it renewed hope and determination. He was seemingly everywhere—giving financial credit, writing rules and regulations for the colony, dispensing advice, dealing with Mexican officials, and organizing raids against marauding Indians.

Ironically, the very fact that Austin's families were educated and hardworking held the seeds of destruction for the Texas dream. These were independent people used to living on their own, with a built-in resentment toward authority. They were not inclined to listen to a faraway government in distant Mexico City, especially when that government continually changed leaders and policies because of almost constant turmoil in the Mexican political system.

The Americans also had little intention of forgetting their prior beliefs and becoming good Mexicans. They brought their own ideas about politics, morals, religion, and business, and they did not want to exchange those ideas for new ones.

In April 1824, Texas was combined with the neighboring Mexican state of Coahuila to become the state of Coahuila y Tejas. At the time it seemed to make sense; Texas as yet had neither the population nor the financial strength to support itself on its own. But what the move actually did was shift local control of Texas affairs to Saltillo, the capital of Coahuila, almost 500 miles away from civilization in Texas. Little noticed by either Austin or the colonists at the time, the combination of the two states and loss of local control would emerge as the single most contentious issue pitting Texas against Mexico.

The first crack in the wall of obedience toward Mexico came in late 1826, when a group of Texas settlers declared independence and created a new republic called Fredonia. Fredonia survived for only a month, but it was a bad sign for Mexico.

As the 1820s ended, more and more Americans were flooding into Texas daily. Some came with an *empresario* as part of a settlers'

People moved to Texas from all over. It offered a fresh start and cheap land in abundance.

colony, but others came on their own. There was nothing to stop them from crossing the border into the state. "A person may travel all day; and day after day, and find Americans only,"[5] wrote one settler about Texas at this time. What helped fuel the exodus was a Mexican law that protected Texas settlers from losing their land or tools for nonpayment of debts in a foreign country. Whenever a person in the United States became trapped in debt, he could just move to Texas with the knowledge that no creditor could seize his land or belongings if he were tracked down. The defiant phrase "Gone to Texas"[6] or just the initials "G.T.T."[7] began popping up on cabin doors throughout the nation, as men deep in debt simply uprooted themselves and their families for a fresh start in Texas.

Alexis de Tocqueville was a French historian who toured America. He wrote his impressions in a book called Democracy in America.

By 1830, there were an estimated 16,000 Americans in Texas—nearly five times as many, with their slaves, as there were Spanish-speaking inhabitants. The Mexicans feared they were in danger of being overrun in Texas by the very people they had initially hoped would save the area for them.

"The province of Texas is still under Mexican rule, but soon there will, so to say, be no more Mexicans there," wrote Alexis de Tocqueville, a Frenchman touring America at the time.

Trying desperately to avoid just that situation, the Mexican government, on April 6, 1830, passed a law forbidding any further immigration from the United States into Texas. They also suspended any further *empresario* contracts.

The Mexicans hoped that the new law would stop Texas from slipping away from them. Instead, it just hastened the arrival of the Texas Revolution.

Stephen Austin

Initially a failure in every venture he tried, Stephen Austin eventually became a famous American and a founder of Texas, which now names its capital city for him.

Stephen Fuller Austin was born on November 3, 1793, in Virginia, and grew up in the Missouri Territory. His father, Moses, was a strong-willed man, and it was impressed on Stephen early and often that his first and most important duty was to his family.

Moses had initially been wealthy, but bad business decisions and economic forces combined to gradually strip the family of its fortune. Moses, however, thought that he saw a way to recapture his wealth and prestige by leading a colony of American families into Texas. He died in June of 1821 before he was able to accomplish his goal. He made it clear, however, that he needed Stephen to take his place and return the Austin family to glory in Texas.

Stephen had tried and failed at careers as a mine operator, merchant, and businessman. At the time of his father's death, he was in New Orleans studying to become a lawyer. Yet he took his father's place, led the first group of 300 families into Texas, and never looked back. By 1835, the more than 1,500 families that Austin settled in Texas had chopped more wood, cleared more land, and raised more crops than the Spanish had in 300 years of trying to settle Texas.

Stephen Austin

Of all the *empresarios*, Austin was the best. He took a deep and paternal interest in his colony, acting as a father, policy-maker, and diplomat all in one. Mexican politics frequently changed rulers and philosophies during the 1820s and early 1830s. Through all the turbulence Austin was a calming voice, repeatedly calling for patience and loyalty to Mexico even while more radical colonists advocated independence.

That all changed in 1834, after he was imprisoned by Santa Anna. Austin became a full-blown revolutionary, initially leading the fight against Mexico. But he was no military man, and others with more experience, like Sam Houston, quickly superseded him.

Always frail, Austin wore himself out through overwork. He died on December 27, 1836, at the age of 43.

FYI For Your Information

When Mexican troops came to reclaim a cannon, Texians defended it. The incident helped push Texas into war with Mexico.

Chapter

The Texas Revolution

Like a slowly building fire, the Texas Revolution finally exploded into white-hot fury in December 1835. Yet surprisingly, within a few months the struggle had ended, and Texas became free and independent.

The Mexican law of April 6, 1830, which barred further American immigration into Texas, ignited the smoldering embers of rebellion that had been present just below the surface there.

"A more impolitic measure could not have been adopted by this Government,"[1] said Austin upon learning of the law. He knew that the law would provide those who agitated for more independence from Mexico with a powerful new argument. They could claim, with some justification, that Mexico did not trust them, and was attempting to isolate them by stopping other Americans from entering Texas.

Shortly thereafter, the government established a new military post at Anahuac, a small community on the northern end of Galveston Bay. In April 1832, soldiers were sent from there to stop the tarring and feathering of a Texas man who had witnessed a brutal attack and did nothing to stop it. The Texians resented having the Mexicans interfere in their business, and shots were fired between the two groups. It was a harbinger of much worse to come.

One of those involved in the Anahuac affair was a fiery young lawyer named William Barret Travis, formerly of South Carolina. He had abandoned his wife and child there because of crushing debt and, like many a man, had come to Texas to start over.

Another man who was beginning to play a role in Texas affairs was an adventurer named James Bowie. In August 1832, he led an outnumbered group of Texians to victory over Mexican soldiers near Nacogdoches. Both Travis and Bowie were beginning to emerge as leaders in the Texas demand for individual statehood and more control over local affairs.

Austin realized that events were spinning away from him. He decided to run for president of a convention that was called in October 1832 in the Texas town of San Felipe. The convention would request more self-government for Texas and convince Santa Anna (the apparent winner in yet another Mexican government revolution) of Texian loyalty. Running for president was the only way he now could stay ahead of developments. He won the election, defeating the more radical William H. Wharton.

Because of the chaotic nature of events in Mexico, that convention's documents and expressions of loyalty never arrived in Mexico City. In the meantime, Santa Anna had indeed won control of the Mexican government. So on April 1, 1833, yet another Texas self-government convention was held—but this one was very different from the first. This convention elected Wharton president, and took the bold step of writing a constitution for the State of Texas. Among those who helped write the document was Sam Houston—another person who had recently moved to Texas. The convention selected Austin to bring the constitution directly to Mexico City and Santa Anna.

Austin realized that drafting a constitution for a single state of Texas was practically like slapping Mexican authorities in the face with their demands for self-government. Yet he also knew that many in Texas doubted his allegiance to the American settlers. He reluctantly agreed to go to Mexico City—a difficult journey of nearly 1,000 miles.

The seven-week trip was rough, and an exhausted Austin arrived to find Mexico City in the grip of a cholera epidemic that had killed close to 20,000 and caused many to flee. Any Mexican officials he found in the city firmly dismissed his pleas for Texas.

Mexico City was a strange place for an American at that time. With a population of nearly 200,000, soaring cathedrals, elegant plazas, and beautiful homes with fountain courtyards, it was a worldly European-style city bearing little resemblance to the much simpler and less opulent American cities. Ill and depressed, Austin wrote an unguarded letter on October 2 to the San Antonio *ayuntamiento* (local ruling council). "The fate of Texas depends upon itself and not upon this government. The country is lost if its inhabitants do not take its affairs into their own hands,"[2] he said.

It was an unfortunate letter, for it could be—and was—interpreted by jumpy Mexican officials as a call to arms in Texas. Someone in San Antonio sent it to Mexico City, where it outraged officials. By this time Austin had started for home, but the Mexican authorities caught up with him and arrested him on January 3, 1834. He was returned to Mexico City and thrown into prison.

Like the calm before the storm, an eerie peace settled over Texas. Even from prison Austin urged patience, and so did others, such as Houston.

Santa Anna, who now had dictatorial powers, had finally had enough of Mexican states that caused trouble. Zacatecas was another state that had been agitating for more independence; Santa Anna's answer was to send an army to plunder its capital city. The example was clear to Texas: They were next. This was made more apparent when captured Mexican dispatches confirmed that Santa Anna was going to lead his army across Texas to punish the troublesome Americans.

Early in September 1835, Austin finally arrived back in Texas, but now he was a changed man. He had seen Santa Anna up close, and did not like the view. He called him "a base, unprincipled bloody monster."[3] It was, he said, time for all-out war.

Events began to move at a furious pace. On October 2, 1835, 160 Texians surrounded a small brass cannon in the town of Gonzales that 100 Mexican soldiers had come to reclaim. "Come And Take It"[4] read the defiant banner the Texians raised over the cannon. After a short battle, the Mexicans retreated. The Texas Revolution had begun.

In the beginning, the revolution seemed like it was going to be easy for the Texians. On October 9, 1835, they won another victory at Goliad, then Bowie and 90 men defeated a party of 400 Mexican cavalry.

Austin was not a military man, but he accepted the command of the disorganized Texian army of several hundred volunteers anyway. It was very much an army that moved on its own. Santa Anna's brother-in-law, General Martín Perfecto de Cos, had occupied San Antonio with 1,400 troops. The Texas army made its way to San Antonio but, being outnumbered, had no desire to attack well-entrenched troops. Despite attempts by Austin to get them to attack, the army refused to fight and settled down to a siege.

As the warm days of autumn gave way to winter's cold, many in the Texas army began drifting back home. Austin, frustrated, tired, and realizing that he was no military commander, was replaced on November 12, 1835, by the more experienced Edward Burleson. Austin accepted an assignment for the provisional Texas government to raise money and volunteers in the United States.

Still the Texian army wouldn't fight, and no amount of ordering or begging seemed able to get it to move. Finally, early in December, with the army on the verge of walking away from San Antonio, a Texian named Ben Milam pleaded with the men to attack. "Boys! Who will go with Ben Milam into Bexar?"[5] he urged. His words carried the day. On December 5, 1835, they attacked the Mexicans, and after several days of fighting once again won a smashing victory.

This latest triumph touched off celebrations throughout Texas. Believing the job finished, some in the Texas army went home. It seemed that independence was all but assured.

Some other Texians, such as Sam Houston, knew better. They knew that Santa Anna would not give up Texas that easily. They also

Dawn at the Alamo, a 1905 painting by Henry Arthur McArdle, is one of many guesses as to how the battle at the Alamo appeared. Every artist brings his or her own interpretation to the event.

knew that his main army was skilled and dedicated—a far cry from the motley collection of troops the Texians had mainly beaten so far.

Houston, appointed commander-in-chief of the army, was trying hard to organize it while the provisional Texas government bickered over what to do next. Meanwhile, that which Houston feared most was occurring: Santa Anna and over five thousand battle-hardened troops crossed the Rio Grande (Spanish for "Big River") from Mexico into Texas on February 16, 1836, and were roaring toward the Texians on *El Camino Real*—an old Spanish road that cut through the heart of Texas. Their first stop was San Antonio de Béxar.

At Béxar, less than 200 Texians were holed up in a crumbling adobe mission called the Alamo. Although the Texians had tried to turn the building into a fortress, the Alamo complex was too large, and there were too few Texians, for it to be properly defended against an invading army.

Santa Anna meets Sam Houston after San Jacinto. Houston was wounded in the battle, which is why he is reclining.

On February 23, the first units of Mexican troops reached San Antonio, and the Alamo defenders were trapped. "Victory or death,"[6] Texian Commander William Barret Travis grimly wrote as more and more Mexican troops arrived each day.

Unfortunately, it was death. In the predawn hours of March 6, 1836, Santa Anna attacked the Alamo with 4,000 men. In a vicious battle that lasted only ninety minutes, all of the Alamo defenders, including Travis, Bowie, and Davy Crockett, a famous American frontiersman and politician, were killed.

The Alamo battle hardly stopped Santa Anna as he steamed toward the rebellious Texians. They were meeting in a hovel of a town in central Texas called Washington-on-the-Brazos to elect a government and compose a declaration of independence and a constitution for the new nation.

On March 11, Houston learned of the sad fate of the Alamo. Soon after, he began the Runaway Scrape. When 1,100 Mexican soldiers executed several hundred Texian troops at Goliad on March 27, the Runaway Scrape shifted into high gear as everyone scrambled to get out of the Mexican army's way. Santa Anna, not unrealistically, felt that the end was in sight for the Texas Revolution.

Then came the Battle of San Jacinto on April 21. In its aftermath, the world had a new country: the Republic of Texas.

The Battle of the Alamo

Of all the many wars in history, certain battles stand out. Historians revisit them over and over, trying to discover their deeper meaning, while the ordinary person is drawn to them because they touch a chord in the human psyche. The Alamo is such a battle.

Initially the Alamo was not supposed to be held by the Texians. Sam Houston had sent James Bowie there with orders to destroy it and remove its guns. Houston's plans for fighting the vastly superior Mexican army did not include having untrained Texian soldiers try to hold fortresses.

But Bowie was not a true military man. He was an adventurer and a fighter—a born leader of men. When he rode into San Antonio de Béxar on January 19, 1836, and saw the many improvements that had been made in the Alamo's defenses, he felt confident that it could be held.

First Company of Texan Volunteers from New Orleans Flag, captured by Mexican army at the Alamo

Indeed, the defenses of the nearly three-acre compound had been radically improved by twenty-nine-year-old Texian Green Jameson. Most critically, Jameson had built platforms of wood and earth that partially protected the Alamo's sharpshooters and artillerymen as they fired over the twelve-foot-high walls. He had also placed cannon at critical spots and constructed barriers to cover other weaknesses.

To this makeshift fortress came nearly 200 men, among them Bowie, William Barret Travis, and Davy Crockett. All figured that they would inevitably receive reinforcements. Crockett entertained the defenders with his fiddle playing while they waited for help to arrive. But as the days of late February faded into early March and the Mexican force around the Alamo grew, a sense of doom settled over the men trapped inside. The hoped-for reinforcements never showed, and the defenders knew that they could not hold the place with so few men.

Yet they all stayed (except one, according to a famous story that may or may not be true). In the face of certain death, they remained in the Alamo, determined to sell their lives dearly in the cause for Texas's independence. Even though the end, when it came on March 6, took just ninety minutes, the defenders of the Alamo assured that they'd live forever by showing the world what courage, bravery, and devotion to a principle truly mean.

Sam Houston had been a politician and a drunk before he came to Texas. There he became a military leader and a statesman.

Chapter

The Republic of Texas

Improbably, the Texians had won their revolution. Much like the thirteen American colonies a half century before, the Texians had defeated a better-armed, better-organized, and better-equipped foe. But in the wake of the celebrations that followed the Battle of San Jacinto, few Texians bothered to ponder the enormity of the task before them. They were to be not just a state within the protective embrace of a central government, but a completely new country. Everything would have to be made up from scratch.

The first thing to do was elect a president. Stephen Austin, whose spirits had sunk after the Alamo and Goliad but who had never doubted that Texas would persevere in the end, returned from the United States on June 1, 1836. But he was yesterday's hero. He was the one who had long advocated for coexistence with the Mexicans.

Houston was the hero of Texas now, and Austin knew it. "A successful military chieftain is hailed with admiration and applause . . . but the bloodless pioneer of the wilderness . . . attracts no notice,"[1]

Andrew Jackson was the seventh president of the United States. He was in favor of adding Texas to the Union.

he said. This was proven in the election for Texas's first president on September 5, 1836: Houston received 5,119 votes to just 587 for Austin. The man who had single-handedly helped hundreds carve an existence out of the Texas wilderness was now not considered good enough to lead the new country.

To no one's surprise, voters in the election also formed a Texas republic much like the United States: The new Texas nation would be led by a president, and it would have two houses of Congress and a Supreme Court. Its flag contained a single star, and thus Texas became known as the Lone Star Republic.

"As yet our course is onward," said Houston at his inauguration. "We are only in the outset of the campaign of liberty."[2] Realizing what Austin had meant to Texas, Houston made him secretary of state of the new republic.

As secretary of state, Austin delivered his final service for Texas. Exhausted and sick, he would not live out the year. A referendum held in conjunction with the September 5 election showed overwhelming support, by a vote of 3,277 to 93, for Texas to join the United States. Austin hatched a scheme whereby Santa Anna, currently in a Texas prison, would journey to Washington, D.C., as an unofficial Mexican ambassador, and present an unofficial offer to President Andrew Jackson to buy Texas from Mexico.

While Mexico would never officially offer such a plan, because it still considered Texas part of Mexico, Santa Anna could, with the knowledge that he could sell the idea in Mexico City once he returned there. Santa Anna privately admitted that Texas was forever lost to Mexico, and that it could never be retaken without an expenditure of manpower and money that Mexico simply could not afford. Jackson, an aggressive president, was keen to add yet another piece to the growing American nation.

When Jackson and Santa Anna met, the American president unofficially offered $3.5 million for Texas and other Mexican-held territory on the North American continent, including California. Jackson was so eager to send Santa Anna back to Mexico City to begin selling the idea that he provided a warship for the Mexican general to sail back to Mexico.

The very thing that would rip the nation apart in a few decades—slavery—sidetracked Texas's annexation to the United States. Texas allowed slavery, and the growing American abolitionist movement saw a sinister plan by pro-slavery factions to spread slavery by bringing Texas into the Union. Indeed, some, such as former president and current Congressman John Quincy Adams, predicted that the annexation

33

of Texas to the United States would lead to American attempts to seize Cuba, possibly igniting a global war with European nations.

Jackson, who never backed down from a fight, most likely would have gladly battled his enemies over adding Texas to the United States, but his second term as president was ending. Without hearing anything positive from Mexico City about his offer, Jackson simply ran out of time before he was able to do anything about Texas.

Jackson did the only thing he could do. On March 3, 1837, the last day of his term as president, he extended diplomatic recognition to Texas. But annexation—making Texas part of the Union—was a long way off.

Texas would have to go it alone . . . and it was not easy.

The new nation faced many problems. For instance, in the beginning there was no official seal with which to notarize government documents. President Houston found that he had to constantly handwrite on official papers the notation: "Given under my hand and private seal there being no seal of office at Columbia."[3] (Columbia was the capital city.)

The tiny frontier town in southern Texas near the lower Brazos River was ill-suited for being the capital of the new country. Columbia had few buildings, and those that stood were taken over by the Congress. A two-story house served as the home of the House of Representatives, while the smaller Senate met in a one-story dwelling. Senate committees conducted official business in sheds attached to the home. Surrounding the town were woods filled with deer, turkeys, and bears.

Security was another big concern for Texas. The fierce Comanche Indian tribe was raiding and attacking the settlement colonies, taking advantage of the lack of manpower caused by the revolution. Houston, more sympathetic to Native Americans than most people at the time because he had lived with the Cherokee for a few years, tried to end the war by treaty, but found the atmosphere toward the Native Americans too hostile among Texans.

Another security problem came from Mexico. Santa Anna, despite his words to the contrary, still desired Texas, and Mexico refused to recognize Texas's independence. In the spring of 1842, Santa Anna sent a force under General Rafael Vásquez to attack San Antonio. The attack succeeded, but Vásquez retreated back to Mexico after a few days. A few months later another Mexican army attacked San Antonio. This time a Texas army was required to chase the Mexicans back to Mexico.

Coupled with the ongoing problems with the Indians and Mexicans were financial troubles. An economic slowdown called the Panic of 1837 struck the United States that year, and its effects were felt in Texas as well. Conditions got so bad that hard currency—gold and silver—virtually disappeared, and animals such as horses and cows were used as Texas money in a crude barter system. One man used a plot of land to pay for several boxes of cherries for his wife. The scarcity of hard money caused the price of goods to skyrocket.

This economic uncertainty was combined with a government that never had enough money. Because of constant fears of war with Mexico, Texas had to spend large sums on military preparation, lest they get caught unawares. Money that could have been spent on internal improvements, such as better roads, was consumed by the continual need for defense. Thus, Texas roads were made of dirt, prone to becoming muddy and impassible during bad weather. Stagecoach drivers had to carry long, thick poles to push the stage out of the mud when it got stuck. Because of the poor roads, mail service was terrible.

Not all the news in Texas during its years as an independent republic was bad. The population surged upward, from approximately 50,000 to 125,000, as families continued pouring into Texas to take advantage of its cheap, plentiful land. New cities were started, most prominently Houston, named after the republic's first president. The capital had moved there from Columbia in 1837, and Houston grew by leaps and bounds, as did another city fifty miles south, Galveston.

Great industries were started as well. Texas weather and soil were perfect for growing cotton. The cotton crop jumped from 10,000 bales in 1834 to 58,000 bales in 1849. A man named James Taylor White became the first of the Texas cattle barons. He had arrived in Texas with just three cows; by 1842, he owned 30,000 head of cattle.

35

People often traveled by stagecoach in the West. It may not have been comfortable, but it was better than horseback. In Texas, the roads were so poor, stagecoaches would get stuck in the mud.

Still, there was an apprehensive air throughout Texas during this time. The fear that Mexico would attack, along with Indian raids, was a constant worry. This, coupled with economic instability, invariably caused Texians to wonder what had happened to the glorious future that independence had offered.

"A general gloom seems to rest over every section of the Republic," said a Texas newspaper in 1842, "and doubt and sorrow are depicted on almost every brow."[4]

What could be done?

The Council House Tragedy

The feet of Matilda Lockhart were burned by the Comanche Indians

Among the Native American tribes that the Texians had to deal with, none was as feared as the Comanche. A warrior people, the Comanche and Texians fought each other with furious intensity. A treaty between the two sides would have been the logical way to stop the killing. Unfortunately, a terrible incident in San Antonio in 1840 ruined any hope of a treaty.

In January 1840, after a period of brutal warfare between the two sides, three Comanche chiefs showed up in San Antonio and requested a conference for the purpose of hammering out a treaty. Colonel Henry Karnes said that a conference could be held in March at the city's Council House, provided the Indians brought with them all their white captives. Karnes planned a trap for the Comanche in case they didn't comply with his request.

About sixty-five Native Americans showed up in March, but they brought with them just one captive: a fifteen-year-old girl named Matilda Lockhart. Her nose had been burned off down to the bone. According to her, the Comanche had tortured her by repeatedly burning her nose and beating her. She also claimed that she had seen at least fifteen other prisoners. However, when asked why they hadn't brought them along too, the Comanche claimed that the others were the property of other Comanche bands, and that they could not speak for them.

Perhaps this was true; each Comanche group operated independently the others, and no one chief could control another's actions.

True or not, the Texians did not believe the Comanche, and they sprang their trap. A battle broke out between the two sides. When the firing died down, seven Texians and more than thirty-five Indians lay dead.

Predictably, the chance for peace between the two sides died with them. In August, 500 Comanche warriors retaliated. They attacked and wiped out the settlements of Victoria and Linnville.

FYI For Your Information

NO ANNEXATION
OF
TEXAS

It having been announced by the Government organ that a Treaty for the Annexation of Texas has been negociated and signed, and will soon be presented to the Senate, the undersigned call upon the citizens of New York, without distinction of Party, who are opposed to the Ratification of said Treaty, to meet at the Tabernacle, on Monday evening, the 22d of April inst., to express their opposition to the same.

Dated, *New York, April 18th,* 1844.

The annexation of Texas to the Union was a hotly debated topic. For a decade, the issue raged through American politics.

Chapter

Texas Joins the United States

The Texas question—whether or not to admit Texas into the Union—dominated the politics of the United States from almost the moment that Texas won its freedom from Mexico.

Andrew Jackson, president of the United States during the first few months of Texas's independence, had to be careful. He was very much in favor of admitting Texas to the Union, but he had more than his own feelings to consider.

Martin Van Buren, Jackson's friend and vice president, was running for president in 1836. The question of whether or not to admit Texas was a critical issue in the election. Jackson knew that if he recognized Texas, Van Buren would lose the votes of Northerners who were opposed to slavery. It might cost Van Buren the election.

He also could not rush to recognize Texas because Mexico refused to admit that Texas was gone. Jumping in too soon on Texas could provoke a war with Mexico.

So Jackson did nothing. Van Buren swept to victory in the presidential election of 1836. As related in the previous chapter, Jackson extended diplomatic recognition to Texas on March 3, 1837.

CHAPTER 5

John Tyler became president of the United States when Harrison died.

The wily Sam Houston knew that another argument was needed to convince the U.S. government to annex Texas. He found that argument across the Atlantic Ocean, in Great Britain and France. In October 1837, Houston sent J. Pinckney Henderson to both France and England. Henderson's job was supposedly to negotiate for diplomatic recognition and trade agreements with the two countries. What Houston really wanted, however, was to show America that Texas could easily allow two European powers with possible expansionist ideas to establish a major foothold right next to U.S. soil.

But nothing was going to happen concerning annexation as long as Van Buren was president. The Panic of 1837 caused severe economic distress in the United States, and Van Buren's popularity plummeted. Politically weakened, he wasn't about to tackle a controversial issue like the annexation of Texas.

Texas's prospects for American statehood began looking up in the 1840s. William Henry Harrison, elected the ninth president of the United States in November 1840, died one month after taking office. He was succeeded by his vice president, Virginian John Tyler, who supported the annexation of Texas.

Now Houston really went to work. He instructed his representative in Washington to reject any talk of annexation, because it might bother the British. On December 12, 1843, he gave a speech to the Texas Congress in which he praised Great Britain yet barely mentioned the United States. Alarm bells began going off in America. Would Texas really join with the country's old enemy, Great Britain?

The pressure began to build to annex Texas before another country snatched her away. Andrew Jackson warned that America must annex Texas—"peaceably if we can, forcibly if we must."[1]

In April 1844, a treaty of annexation for Texas was presented to the U.S. Senate, which needed a two-thirds majority to approve it. Confident of victory, President Tyler had overestimated the pro-Texas sentiment. The treaty was rejected 35-16.

Houston had warned that if Texas was rejected, the time had come for them to forget the statehood question and "redouble our energies"[2] to make a go of it as an independent nation.

However, Jackson, who by this time was in bad health, was still a powerful political voice urging Texas's annexation. "[A]lthough I know my time is short . . . I love my country, and this subject involves its best interests,"[3] he said.

Before Texas could get too far along the road to becoming a strong independent nation, the American presidential election of 1844 swept into office pro-Texas Democrat James K. Polk. Tyler was heartened by the election, feeling that it reflected the mood of the country. He was determined to add Texas to the Union before his presidential term expired.

However, a treaty for Texas annexation would still not obtain a two-thirds majority to pass the Senate. So Tyler decided to introduce a joint resolution proposing the annexation. It would only have to pass by majority vote.

Former President John Quincy Adams, a leader in the fight against annexation, urged the defeat of the resolution, but the tide was turning. Both the House of Representatives and the Senate passed the resolution. Tyler signed it on March 1, 1845, just a few days before leaving office.

"I not only rejoice, but congratulate my beloved country,"[4] Jackson said.

On February 19, 1846, the Lone Star flag of the Republic of Texas was lowered for the last time. "The Republic of Texas is no more,"[5] declared new governor, J. Pinckney Henderson. It was only fitting that as the flag fluttered down the flagpole, Sam Houston stepped forward to catch it.

The Mexican War

Mexican War battle

When the United States annexed Texas, it angered Mexico, which still considered Texas its territory. In addition, the boundary line that the Texians claimed along their southern border was the Rio Grande, but for years, the established boundary between Mexico and Texas had been the Nueces River, 150 miles farther inland. President Polk sent John Slidell to Mexico to try to negotiate the differences, as well as attempt to buy California and New Mexico. Then a new regime overthrew the old in Mexico, refused to negotiate any further, and prepared for war. When Mexican forces twice crossed the Rio Grande and attacked American troops in the early spring of 1846, America declared war on Mexico in May.

The war lasted until 1848. While short, the war was marked by several big battles, including a bloody assault on Mexico City by American troops. Santa Anna was placed in charge of the Mexican troops, but he could not defeat the American forces. In one of the war's final battles, the struggle for Mexico City in September 1847, Santa Anna fled, just as he had fled at San Jacinto years earlier. Although the Americans were frequently outnumbered, their superiority in weapons helped them win.

The war served as a training ground for many American officers who would later go on to participate in the American Civil War. Robert E. Lee, Ulysses Grant, Stonewall Jackson, and numerous other men who fought for the Union and Confederacy got their "on-the-job training" in the Mexican War.

The American victory at Mexico City ended the fighting. After several months of negotiation, the Treaty of Guadalupe Hidalgo was signed in February 1848 to end the war. Besides keeping Texas, the United States obtained New Mexico and California from Mexico.

Chapter Notes

Chapter 1
The Battle of San Jacinto

1. William C. Davis, *Lone Star Rising: The Revolutionary Birth of the Texas Republic* (New York: Free Press, 2004), p. 245.

2. Ibid., p. 266.

3. Ibid., p. 270.

4. Ibid., p. 271.

5. David Nevin, *The Texans* (New York: Time-Life Books, 1975), p. 137.

6. H. W. Brands, *Lone Star Nation: How a Ragged Army of Volunteers Won the Battle for Texas Independence—and Changed America* (New York: Doubleday, 2004), p. 461.

Chapter 2
Men Without a Country

1. H. W. Brands, *Lone Star Nation: How a Ragged Army of Volunteers Won the Battle for Texas Independence—and Changed America* (New York: Doubleday, 2004), p. 36.

2. David Nevin, *The Texans* (New York: Time-Life Books, 1975), p. 24.

3. James L. Haley, *Texas: An Album of History* (Garden City, New York: Doubleday & Company, 1985), p. 16.

4. Brands, p. 65.

5. William C. Davis, *Lone Star Rising: The Revolutionary Birth of the Texas Republic* (New York: Free Press, 2004), p. 73.

6. Nevin, p. 41.

7. Ibid.

8. Davis, p. 76.

Chapter 3
The Texas Revolution

1. H. W. Brands, *Lone Star Nation: How a Ragged Army of Volunteers Won the Battle for Texas Independence—and Changed America* (New York: Doubleday, 2004), p. 156.

2. David Nevin, *The Texans* (New York: Time-Life Books, 1975), p. 68.

3. James L. Haley, *Texas: An Album of History* (Garden City, New York: Doubleday & Company, 1985), p. 33.

4. Brands, p. 263.

5. Ibid., p. 297.

6. Nevin, p. 98.

Chapter 4
The Republic of Texas

1. H. W. Brands, *Lone Star Nation: How a Ragged Army of Volunteers Won the Battle for Texas Independence—and Changed America* (New York: Doubleday, 2004), p. 474.

2. James L. Haley, *Sam Houston* (Norman, Oklahoma: University of Oklahoma Press, 2002), p. 166.

3. Ibid., p. 168.

4. Brands, p. 499.

Chapter 5
Texas Joins the United States

1. David Nevin, *The Texans* (New York: Time-Life Books, 1975), p. 218.

2. James L. Haley, *Sam Houston* (Norman: University of Oklahoma Press, 2002), p. 280.

3. H. W. Brands, *Lone Star Nation: How a Ragged Army of Volunteers Won the Battle for Texas Independence—and Changed America* (New York: Doubleday, 2004), p. 505.

4. Ibid., p. 508.

5. Nevin, p. 219.

Chronology

1800	The Treaty of San Ildefonso transfers the Louisiana Territory to France from Spain.
1803	Napoleon Bonaparte sells the Louisiana Territory to the United States for $15 million.
1806	Zebulon Pike builds an outpost on the Rio Grande, which he mistakes for the Red River. A Spanish patrol discovers him and takes him to the border of Louisiana and Tejas (Texas) so that he can reenter the United States.
1819	The United States gives up all claims to Texas in a treaty with Spain that gives Florida to the United States.
1821	American Moses Austin receives a land grant to settle 300 families in sparsely populated Texas to help deter others from entering Texas with dreams of empire. Moses Austin dies before putting his Texas colonization plan into action. Mexico wins independence from Spain.
1823	Stephen Austin sets up first American colony in Texas along the San Antonio River.
1826	The Fredonia Rebellion signals a widening rift between American settlers in Texas and Mexico.
1828	The border between the United States and Mexico is set at the Sabine River.
1830	Mexico bans further immigration into Texas from the United States.
1832	American settlers in Texas hold a convention at which they vote to make Texas a separate state.
1833	A second pro-statehood convention for Texas is held. Austin brings the convention's documents to Mexico City.
1834	Austin is arrested and imprisoned for one year.
1835	The Texians defend a small brass cannon at the Gonzales settlement against Mexican soldiers who have come to reclaim it, beginning the Texas Revolution.
1835	Victories at Goliad, Concepción, and San Antonio de Béxar give Texas hope that Mexico has been defeated.
1836	
January	James Bowie decides to hold the Alamo, a crumbling adobe mission in Béxar, instead of evacuating it.
February	Main units of Mexican dictator Santa Anna's army cross the Rio Grande and head for Béxar.
March	The Runaway Scrape begins.
March 2	Texian convention at Washington-on-the-Brazos declares independence from Mexico.
March 6	Alamo falls to Santa Anna.
March 27	Surrender and massacre of James Fannin's troops at Goliad.
March–April	Houston continues to retreat across Texas with his army as Santa Anna pursues.
April	Battle of San Jacinto results in an overwhelming Texian victory and Texas independence.
September	Sam Houston is elected first president of Texas.
December	Stephen Austin dies.
1837	U.S. President Andrew Jackson extends diplomatic recognition to Texas.
1840	The Council House tragedy worsens the warfare between Texians and the Comanche tribe.
1841	John Tyler, a supporter of Texas's annexation to the Union, succeeds to the presidency upon the death of William Henry Harrison.

1842	Mexico attacks San Antonio.

1844

April	Treaty of annexation for Texas is voted down in the U.S. Senate.
November	Expansionist James K. Polk is elected president of the United States.

1845	President John Tyler signs a congressional joint resolution annexing Texas to the United States. Mexico breaks off diplomatic relations with the United States in anger over the Texas annexation.
1846	The Mexican War begins; it ends in 1848 with the United States victorious over Mexico.
1861	Texas joins the Confederate States of America.
1863	Sam Houston dies.
1883	Texas purchases the Alamo to preserve it as a historic shrine.

Timeline in History

1775	American Revolution starts.
1776	Declaration of Independence is issued.
1781	General Cornwallis surrenders to George Washington at Yorktown.
1789	French Revolution begins.
1796	George Washington gives his farewell address.
1799	George Washington dies.
1807	Robert E. Lee is born.
1812	War of 1812 begins.
1815	Napoleon Bonaparte is defeated at Waterloo.
1818	Mary Shelley writes *Frankenstein*.
1821	First American colonists go to Texas.
1828	Noah Webster writes *American Dictionary of English Language*.
1837	Samuel Morse invents the telegraph.
1843	First Christmas cards are designed and sent.
1845	Alexander Cartwright helps establish the modern rules of baseball.
1846	Elias Howe patents the sewing machine.
1848	James Marshall discovers gold in California.
1851	Herman Melville publishes *Moby-Dick*.
1856	Gail Borden patents condensed milk.
1857	Currier & Ives begins making prints.
1859	Oil is discovered in Pennsylvania.
1861	The American Civil War begins.
1863	Thanksgiving Day is declared an official holiday.
1867	William "Candy" Cummings throws baseball's first curveball.
1871	The Great Chicago Fire kills 300 people.
1876	The telephone is patented.
1879	Thomas Edison discovers a filament material for his electric lightbulb.
1881	Billy the Kid is killed in New Mexico.
1886	The Statue of Liberty is dedicated.

Further Reading

For Young Adults

Bredeson, Carmen. *Texas*. New York: Children's Press, 2002.

Bredeson, Carmen, and Mary Dodson Wade. *Texas: Celebrate the States*. New York: Benchmark Books, 2005.

Doeden, Matt. *The Battle of the Alamo*. Illustrated by Barnett Charles III and Phil Miller. Mankato, Minnesota: Capstone Press, 2005.

Edmondson, J. R. *Jim Bowie: Frontier Legend, Alamo Hero*. New York: PowerPlus Books, 2003.

Harmon, Daniel E. *Davy Crockett*. Philadelphia: Chelsea House Publishers, 2002.

Hanson-Harding, Alexandra. *Texas*. New York: Children's Press, 2001.

Johnston, Marianne. *Davy Crockett*. New York: PowerKids Press, 2001.

Murphy, Jim. *Inside the Alamo*. New York: Delacorte Press, 2003.

Sasek, Miroslav. *This Is Texas*. New York: Universe Publishing, 2006.

Tanaka, Shelley. *A Day that Changed America: The Alamo*. Illustrated by David Craig. New York: Hyperion Books for Children, 2003.

Wade, Mary Dodson. *Uniquely Texas*. Chicago: Heinemann Library, 2004.

Works Consulted

Brands, H. W. *Lone Star Nation: How a Ragged Army of Volunteers Won the Battle for Texas Independence—and Changed America*. New York: Doubleday, 2004.

Cantrell, Gregg. *Stephen F. Austin—Empresario of Texas*. New Haven, Connecticut: Yale University Press, 1999.

Davis, William C. *Lone Star Rising: The Revolutionary Birth of the Texas Republic*. New York: Free Press, 2004.

———. *Three Roads to the Alamo: The Lives and Fortunes of David Crockett, James Bowie, and William Barret Travis*. New York: HarperCollins, 1998.

Fehrenbach, T. R. *Lone Star: A History of Texas and the Texans*. New York: The Macmillan Company, 1968.

Haley, James L. *Sam Houston*. Norman, Oklahoma: University of Oklahoma Press, 2002.

———. *Texas: An Album of History*. Garden City, New York: Doubleday & Company, 1985.

Nevin, David. *The Texans*. New York: Time-Life Books, 1975.

Nofi, Albert A. *The Alamo and the Texas War for Independence*. Conshohocken, Pennsylvania: Combined Publishing, 1992.

On the Internet

The Alamo
http://www.thealamo.org

Barker, Eugene C., and James W. Pohl. "Texas Revolution"
http://www.tsha.utexas.edu/handbook/online/articles/view/TT/qdt1.html

Digital History
http://www.digitalhistory.uh.edu

Famous Texans: *Sam Houston*
http://www.famoustexans.com/samhouston.htm

Lone Star Junction
http://www.lsjunction.com

Sons of Dewitt Colony, Texas: *Antonio López de Santa Anna*
http://www.tamu.edu/ccbn/dewitt/santaanna.htm

Glossary

afterglow
(AF-tur-gloh)
The pleasant memories of a past
experience.

annex
(AA-neks)
To add, especially to something more
important.

canebrake
(KAYN-brayk)
A long plant with a hollow stem, such as
bamboo.

contentious
(kun-TEN-shus)
Argumentative.

destitute
(DES-tih-toot)
Needy or poor.

exodus
(EK-soh-dus)
A huge movement of people from one
place to another.

harbinger
(HAR-bin-jur)
Anything that predicts a future event.

herald
(HAYR-uld)
To announce.

hovel
(HUH-vul)
A small, beat-up dwelling.

impolitic
(im-PAH-lih-tik)
Unwise.

inept
(in-EPT)
Unfit; unequipped for a job; foolish.

marauding
(mah-RAH-ding)
Thieving, raiding.

motley
(MOT-lee)
An odd group.

notarize
(NOH-tuh-ryz)
To certify through a notary public.

opulent
(AHP-yoo-lent)
Rich; fancy.

persevere
(pur-seh-VEER)
To push through to the end, despite
obstacles.

plunder
(PLUN-dur)
To rob of goods or valuables by force.

poised
(POYZD)
Ready, prepared.

prone
(PROHN)
Having a natural tendency toward.

psyche
(SY-kee)
The human spirit.

supersede
(soo-pur-SEED)
To replace in power or authority.

Texsian
(TEK-see-in)
A person who lived in Texas before it
became a state.

wily
(WY-lee)
Clever.

wrest
(REST)
To take by violence, force, or hard work.

zealot
(ZEL-ut)
A fanatic.

Index